MORE FROM A E

Image Performance
Mat Marquis

Webfont Handbook
Bram Stein

Animation at Work
Rachel Nabors

Color Accessibility Workflows
Geri Coady

Making Sense of Color Management
Craig Hockenberry

Working the Command Line
Remy Sharp

Pricing Design
Dan Mall

Get Ready for CSS Grid Layout
Rachel Andrew

Visit abookapart.com for our full list of titles.

Copyright © 2018 Scott Kubie
All rights reserved

Publisher: Jeffrey Zeldman
Designer: Jason Santa Maria
Editor-in-Chief: Katel LeDû
Managing Editor: Lisa Maria Martin
Copyeditor: Katel LeDû
Proofreader: Mary van Ogtrop
Book Producer: Ron Bilodeau

ISBN: 978-1-937557-79-9

A Book Apart
New York, New York
http://abookapart.com

TABLE OF CONTENTS

1 | *Introduction*

8 | CHAPTER 1
Prepare

24 | CHAPTER 2
Compose

33 | CHAPTER 3
Edit

48 | CHAPTER 4
Finish

57 | *Acknowledgments*

58 | *Resources*

62 | *References*

64 | *Index*

FOREWORD

PLAYING THE PIANO WELL requires more than just technical skill, more than learning to press the right keys at the right moments. It also requires learning how to practice—that is, developing the habits to internalize those technical skills.

The same is true for words. Assembling them in just the right way takes practice. The book you're about to read isn't a guide for putting words together; it's a guide for how to *practice* writing. It's a manual for cultivating good writing habits.

Writing is a process, one that's difficult to articulate precisely. It's equal parts instinct and rote procedure, and Scott helps us navigate both. Like any good recipe, *Writing for Designers* is never definitive, immutable, or exhaustive. It's a starting point, overflowing with tools, techniques, and myriad ways to approach each step in the writing process.

Our design process is fraught with words: words are used to document our ideas, to plan usability tests, to validate color choices. Words are used to prompt, cajole, warn, alert, explain, instruct, and reassure our users. They're an essential building block in the user experience, and we, as designers, can't ignore their power.

Writing for Designers will help you get more comfortable wielding that power in your design process. From getting version control right to tapping into your most creative self, let Scott show you the art and practice of writing.

—Dan Brown

INTRODUCTION

SHIT. THE WRITING. We forgot about the writing. The thing, the design thing…it needs words! Oh man, so many words. I thought somebody…wasn't the client going to…shit. We've got to get the writing done. We've got to get the writing done! How are we going to get the writing done?!

Don't worry, friend. I'm here. We'll get the writing done. The first step is to accept a hard truth: *someone* has to do the writing.

Some teams seem to build their whole process around *not* writing. They fill wireframes with *lorem ipsum* (that fake Latin text that confuses stakeholders) and write *CTA goes here* on their buttons. I've been handed my share of comps where anything remotely word-based was represented by a bunch of squiggly lines.

You know that comic about how to draw an owl? Step one: draw some circles. Step two: draw the rest of the fucking owl. That's you with your squiggly lines. Rude.

Everything left unwritten is a mystery box of incomplete design. These mysteries beget other mysteries, and pretty soon you've got dozens of screens of things that kinda-sorta-*maybe* make sense but none of them can really be final because *you never wrote the words*.

Choosing words and *writing* what appears in an interface forces us to name components, articulate choices, and explain things to the user. It's part of design.

We know this, don't we? We knew it at the beginning of the design project, and yet here we are. Why did we wait?

Writing is part of design

Words are one of the most *powerful* design materials available. They convey deeply complex meanings in a compact space. They load fast. They're easy to manipulate and easy to transmit. And the best part is, you don't have to invent any of them! You just have to use them.

Sometimes words get written off (see what I did there) as mere "details" in our designs. True details can wait until the end of your design process. Words, however, are deeply integrated throughout the user's experience of your design. Look at your favorite app, site, or interface. Take all the words away and what do you have? Not much!

Even if the particular thing you're designing seems light on words, take a broader view and you'll find words hiding everywhere:

- error messages and recovery flows
- confirmation screens
- user-visible metadata like page titles and search engine descriptions
- transactional emails
- in-app user assistance
- support documentation
- changelogs
- feature descriptions and marketing copy

These are as much a part of the design as the layout, graphics, and animations. Designs *depend* on words.

Even if your design were simple, beautiful, and intuitive, writing can take it one step further. Writing can reinforce how you want users to think about your design. Writing can explain the approach or philosophy that underpins your design. Writing can guide users through complex processes. Writing can even help cover for the quirks and compromises in our designs—hopefully not our first resort, but valuable nonetheless.

Sometimes the writing isn't done because we're trying to solve everything with "pure design." Supposed UX thought leaders throw around baloney like "Good design doesn't need explanation" and "If you have to use words, you've failed." Come on. I hope my pilot knows what all those switches in the cockpit do, but I also hope they're labeled, just in case.

To keep things simple in this book, we'll be talking about three general categories of writing you might have to do to support your design work:

- **Interface copy:** Often referred to as UI copy or microcopy, this is the text that's *deeply* integrated within the interface, like labels for form fields, text on buttons, navigation labels

on a website, error messages, and similar. It's often made of single words or short phrases. If the interface would "break" or be extremely hard to use if you removed this text, we'll call it interface copy.
- **Product copy:** Writing that's integral to the function of the site/product/app/experience, but not necessarily a direct part of the interface—the body of an onboarding email, for instance, or a description of updates to an application in a changelog. This is content focused on helping/supporting the reader.
- **Marketing copy:** Longer-form writing that is primarily filling a sales or promotional sort of role. This is content focused on persuading the reader.

Depending on your product and organization, you might have many more buckets of content, or you may find the lines especially blurry even between these three. That's okay! These buckets will just make things easier while we talk about writing in this book. Cool? Cool.

(Oh, and "copy" is just a way to distinguish words written by a designer from the more generic idea of "text," which could be just about anything in your system, including user-generated input.)

Writing is always hard

If you know someone who makes writing look easy, you're right. They make it *look* easy. You can't plan well for a difficult journey if you assume it's going to be an easy journey. Accepting that writing is hard is an important step toward making it easier and getting it done.

Writing is hard because it's personal. Even if you're writing about something you don't feel strongly about, or even something you disagree with, it's still *your* writing. The words you write carry a little echo of you. To get the writing done, you're going to have to be a little vulnerable. Maybe a lot.

Writing is even hard for writers—and since most people don't realize that, they make it even harder on writers. They don't give writers enough time to write. They don't provide enough information to work with. They say things that minimize the difficulty of the task and the skill required to complete it. "You're so creative! This should be easy, right? Shoot me something back before lunch." Ugh.

Unfortunately, there's no special potion you can take to help you get the writing done, and even the most beautifully retro hipster typewriter still needs *you* to operate the keys.

Workflow gets the writing done

So if magic won't help you get the writing done, what will? In design contexts, a useful way to think about writing is *workflow*. Workflow is a big-picture idea that accommodates all kinds of different processes, techniques, and tools.

If following a recipe is a process, making dinner is a workflow. A dinner-making workflow has obvious phases—plan the meal, prep the ingredients, mix and cook things, finish and serve the meal. The specific steps and outcomes vary depending on the meal, but the basic workflow remains the same.

This is also a useful way to think about design writing. No matter what you're cooking up—no matter how custom the request and how many dietary restrictions your stakeholders might have—you'll follow the same basic workflow each time you do the writing:

1. Prepare (to write)
2. Compose (the words)
3. Edit (what you wrote)
4. Finish (the damn writing)

Planning your workflow means choosing the tools, techniques, people, and processes that will be part of each of these four phases. Until this framework becomes old hat, I recommend explicitly planning your writing workflow. Planning is how you avoid getting stuck. You might not immediately know every single tool, step, and person you'll need to get the writing done. But knowing even a few things, and giving yourself a basic map to follow to get the writing done, will help you learn what's missing.

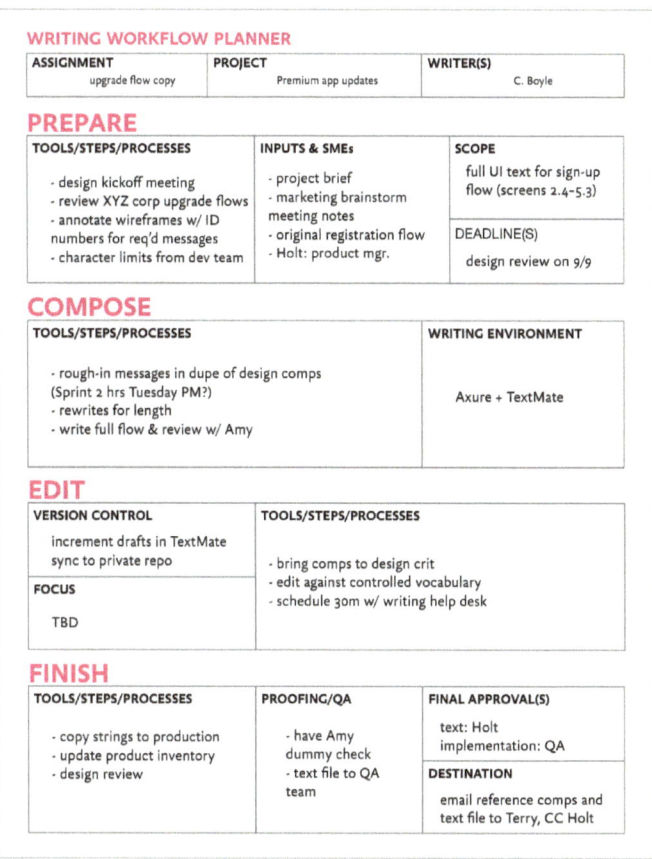

FIG 0.1: A structured worksheet can help you plan your writing workflow before you start, and serve as an anchor in the storm throughout the project. If you go this route, I recommend customizing it to suit the particulars of your organization.

Planning your workflow doesn't need to be a long process — or even something you share with other people. You can create a formal, structured worksheet to plan it out (**FIG 0.1**), you could sketch it out on a whiteboard or in a notebook (**FIG 0.2**), or simply make some notes at the top of a new document. The important thing is to think about *how* you're going to get the writing done before you start writing.

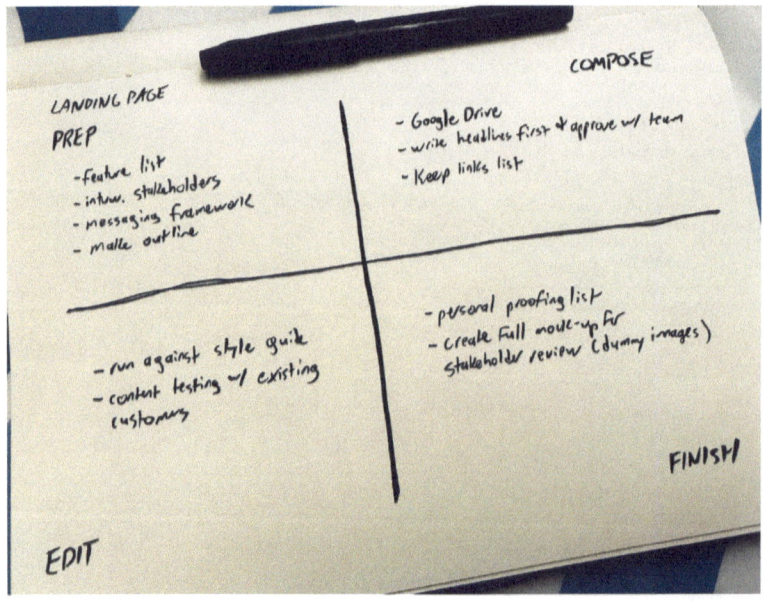

FIG 0.2: Planning your workflow on paper doesn't have to take long, and it's a nice break from staring at screens. Plus, you can cross things off as you go! (Always satisfying.)

You can write

Mr. Hays, my high school choir teacher, was a great recruiter. When he'd ask people to try out for choir, they'd protest with some version of "Oh, no, I can't sing." Nonsense, he'd say: "If you can talk, you can sing. It's all the same muscles!" And, more often than not, he'd pull that student right over to a piano and demonstrate to them that they could, in fact, sing.

In case you're skeptical, worried, or unsure about whether or not you can handle this, here's my pitch for writing: writing is just thinking plus typing. You can think. You can type (or otherwise get text into a computer). So yes, you can write.

We're going to get into all kinds of methods about how to compose and refine text throughout this book. But at the end of the day, writing is just thinking plus typing. Have some thoughts in your head, then write them down. Do this over and over until the writing is done. Every other tip, trick, method, and process is just an improvement or distillation of this basic approach.

And more good news: writing is more like design than you might think. Common design activities like framing the problem, identifying constraints, and exploring solutions are part of writing, too. Many of the methodologies one might use in UX work can be part of a writing workflow: stakeholder interviews, user research, content auditing, ideation workshops, critiques, and more.

Writing is always hard, yes. But it gets easier.

Good? Good. We're making progress already. It's time to Prepare.

PREPARE

THERE'S MORE TO WRITING THAN WRITING, especially when it's part of design. It's easier to get the writing done when you thoughtfully and intentionally *prepare* to do the writing. Smart writers do prep work on every assignment. You can be smart, too!

Whether you've got just a few strings to write for a new screen in your app, or a whole site full of marketing content, you'll want to do each of the following in order to fully prepare to get the writing done:

- articulate the assignment
- collect inputs
- generate ideas
- create structure
- make space to write

You might be feeling an instinct to rush past this phase, especially if you need those words, like, yesterday. But the more time you're able to spend here, the faster and more successful the remaining phases of your writing workflow will be. As Abraham Lincoln once said to Albert Einstein at Mark Twain's birthday party: If you've only got six hours to chop down a cherry tree, spend five hours sharpening your samurai sword. (I think that's the quote, anyway.)

ARTICULATE THE ASSIGNMENT

How are you supposed to get the writing done if you don't know what needs doing? What kinds of words? Where? For what purpose? What will it mean to be *done* with the writing? And what's your role in all this, anyway?

To answer these questions, you need to articulate your *writing assignment*. A design could require one big writing assignment, or lots of little ones. (Or lots of big ones. Or a mix!) The assignment is a flexible unit that says, "Here are the boundaries of the writing work I am responsible for."

Design writing assignments vary, of course, but tend to share some common characteristics:

- **Deadline**: When does the writing assignment—independent of the rest of the design project—need to be completed? This deadline could be something you work into the overall project plan, along with a schedule for check-ins and reviews.
- **Roles**: Your whole team needs a shared understanding of what it means to be the writer. What resources are available to writers? What expectations apply to writers? Are you responsible for getting a draft together for someone else to refine, or do you need to fully own the text? Take nothing for granted, especially the first time.
- **Context**: Where will the writing go? Who will be reading it? What are the circumstances of their reading it? You may feel like you know all of this from the design work already, but often a particular bit of writing (like an error message or confirmation dialog) will be specific to a subset of users or situations.
- **Requirements/Constraints**: What specific requirements and constraints apply to this writing? Are there character limits? Things that have to be mentioned for legal or practical reasons? Controlled vocabularies for interface elements?
- **Scope**: Scope is the checklist of all the "stuff" you have to actually write. Scope could be as simple as a description of the page and an outline of points you need to make, or it could be a complex inventory of messages required by an interactive experience.

Taken together, your deadline, role, context, requirements, and scope will give you a complete idea of what you need to do to be *done*. That's your assignment.

Err on the side of capturing this information publicly, even if it seems like no one else cares, just to cover your butt. The header area of a task or ticket in your project management system is a great option, or even just an email to your team: "Hey friends, here's what I understand about the writing needs on this project. Let me know if I've missed anything…"

This is a good gut-check moment. Does the assignment seem right? Good? Doable? In articulating your assignment, you might have already learned that what seemed like one assignment could be better managed as several. Or that the scope is just too darn big given the deadlines you need to hit. Do what you can to work out these kinks *before* you start writing to save time for everyone (but mostly you).

COLLECT INPUTS

Writing in design can feel more like assembling a puzzle than writing a novel—and someone's ripped open twenty puzzles at once and dumped all the pieces together. Worry about sorting and choosing the right pieces later. First, just make sure you *have* all of the pieces. You want to collect *inputs*.

If the people asking you to do the writing are not writers, they may not have any idea what would be useful to you. And you might not know what's useful until you see it. Ask stakeholders for all of the material they have relating to the project, even if they're not sure it's relevant.

At my company, we call this the "document dump." And sometimes it's a real dump, all right. But every junk yard has its treasures. Some good stuff to ask for:

- notes from meetings, interviews, and workshops
- project briefs and scope of work documents
- design comps, wireframes, and task flows
- marketing collateral
- user personas and research findings

If you know early on that you're going to be the writer on a project, take a fresh look at the calendar for any meetings or research sessions that might be valuable to sit in on. Many teams don't think to invite writers to these things. Being there in person (and doing your own interviews, if you have time) allows you to record what people actually say and how they say it—there's often a lot of flavor in how people speak that doesn't make it into a project manager's notes, but can be very valuable when it comes to doing the writing.

As you collect all of these things, be sure to keep your receipts. Track your inputs and where they came from. For a huge project with lots of inputs, you could go full spreadsheet, but descriptive file names and a few notes scribbled here and there might be enough. Later on in the project, you'll be grateful to have a paper trail, so to speak, as reviewers and stakeholders start asking questions and trying to poke holes in your writing. (It's okay—that's their job!)

Tracking inputs is especially important if you're able to reuse text that's already been through things like legal and compliance reviews. Two of the questions you'll hear most often about writing are: "Who else has looked at this?" and "Where did this [copy/phrase/slogan/benefit/feature/wording] come from?"

GENERATE IDEAS

Now we're closing in on where most people start their writing work—coming up with ideas. It's important to separate the action of generating ideas from doing the writing: first think, then write.

When you're generating ideas, anything is possible. The words are made up and the rules don't matter! This open mindset is necessary for creativity to flourish, as you've probably found in your design work. Treating the words in your design like annoying tasks that are in your way is not a mindset that lends itself to thoughtful, useful, and/or creative writing.

There are lots of ways to generate ideas for design writing. Some are going to work very well for your assignment, and some might not fit at all. I'm going to cover a few methods that work well in many situations.

Mindmapping

Most writing tools don't make thinking easy. When writers start generating ideas inside a blank document in Microsoft Word, or a blank body field in their CMS, they're literally doing their thinking inside of a box.

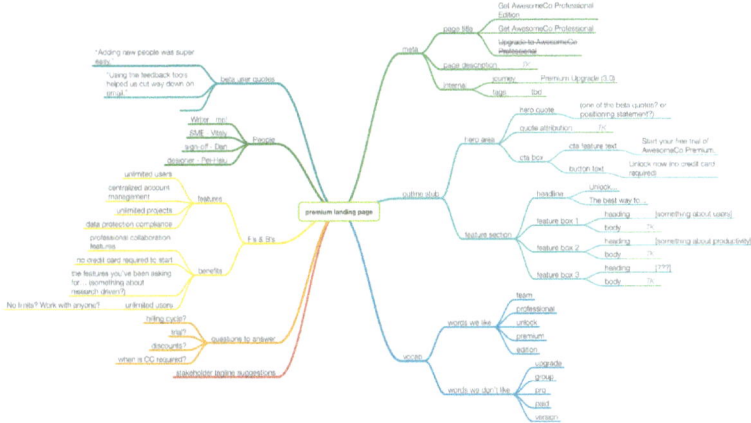

FIG 1.1: Marketing and product content often present many different paths for communicating the same idea. A mindmap encourages you to capture those options as they occur to you and keep moving, rather than debating them in your head.

Mindmapping breaks you out of that box. A mindmap is a visual outline that offers a flexible, nonlinear way of brainstorming and organizing your thoughts. You may have found yourself intuitively creating a mindmap when standing in front of a whiteboard or while scratching out ideas on a napkin.

For marketing and product content, mindmaps are great for transitioning from a big mess of ideas into a linear outline. You can start mashing together snippets of writing, recycled text, quotes, and any other random notion you have into one single canvas and begin sorting them into sections that make sense (FIG 1.1). For interface content, mindmaps can be a great way to collect and sort ideas for labels and feature names (FIG 1.2). In either case, having a bunch of options collected in one place ensures you'll never experience blank-page paralysis when it's time to do the writing.

Mindmapping makes it easy to start thinking and planning with words in small ways, without committing to *writing* everything at once, like that big, empty New Document window wants you to do.

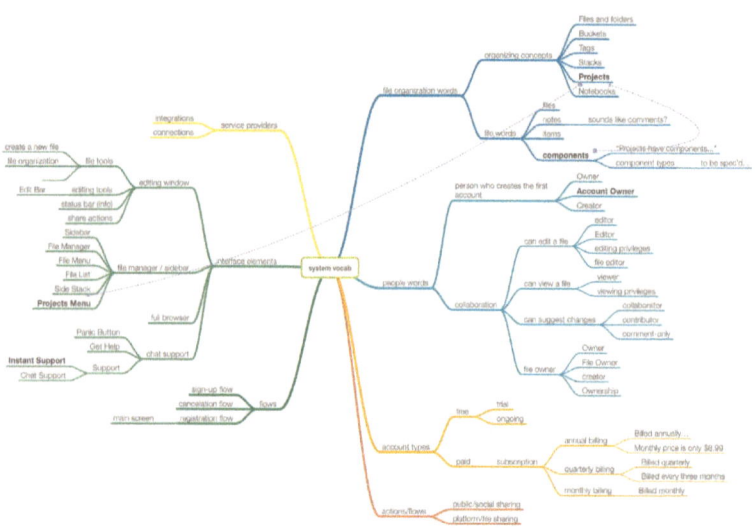

FIG 1.2: Mindmaps can help you make sense of the shape of an interface or workflow, or quickly collect a lot of label options.

Freewriting

Like mindmapping, freewriting is a technique you've probably informally used before. Freewriting is stringing words together for a *set amount of time*. It's especially effective for longform product and marketing copy.

If you want to try freewriting, here are a few things to consider:

- Use a timer, not a clock. If you're watching the clock, you're multitasking. The whole point of this is to *not* multitask—just write.
- Go for quantity, not quality. Try to write as many gosh-dang-doodily words as you can. Typitty type type type, my friend. Remember, this is still just an input—*not* a first draft.
- Fight the urge to switch to planning/designing/outlining. Write down whatever comes into your head, e.g., "Another reason this product is great is that—you know what, I need

to pick up milk from the store—is that it does XYZ faster than the competition." You can pull out the relevant bits to your outline later.

Here's an example of my freewriting for a to-do list application's marketing page:

> *we want you to subscribe to our to-do list software. we want your money please subscribe. go for the premium plan because it's the best value, especially if you sign up for a year. there's also a free forever plan for one device. it's very good software and it gets updated all the time, unlike the other guys who seem to only do a big update every six months. It syncs faster and more reliably than any other app (is that true?). encryption is coming soon and will be added for free when it releases. What are the benefits though how are we different, it's different because you can sync through whatever service you want, it allows you to customize how tags and categories work or not use them at all (it's to-dos done your way? tagline?)*

Obviously—hopefully!—this is not website-ready marketing copy. Even if you cleaned up the sentences, it's still a big blob of text. That's okay—you're just generating ideas. This is a lump of wet clay, and you haven't yet decided if you're going to throw it into one big, beautiful vase or a set of ten tiny teacups.

You can even modify this technique for interface and conversational content with a few simple prefixes:

> *A: What do you want to do today?*
> *B: ummm i want to buy pants I guess.*
> *A: pants are a thing that we sell. see where it says PANTS up there?*
> *B: Pants, got it. Wow that's a big list.*
> *A: Yes. we sell many kinds of pants. Do you want men's or women's pants? Or maybe a certain color?*
> *B: Black pants.*
> *A: Here are all of our black pants.*
> *B: Wow that is a lot of pants. Just show me women's pants.*
> *A: Just women's pants, got it.*

And so on. There are other techniques that will create similar inputs—having users talk aloud during user research sessions, for instance, or pair writing with a partner. Riffing like this can give you a lot to work with when it comes time to distill it down into tidy text for your interface.

Brainstorming

Let's be real: a brainstorming meeting is a meeting where everyone is responsible for generating ideas, which also means that *no one* is responsible for generating ideas—so avoid them if you can.

If there's too much organizational inertia working against you, and you find yourself stuck holding a "Let's brainstorm the writing!" meeting, these tips will make it less painful and more productive:

- Make idea generation the *sole* agenda item. Packing brainstorming into an existing agenda is asking for trouble. It takes a certain amount of time and energy to get into an open frame of mind—anything other than idea generation will pull you closed, hampering both the quantity and quality of your ideation session.
- Avoid decisions of all kinds. Decision-making is a form of convergent thinking. It's an act of limiting, reducing, filtering, choosing—*editing*. Making decisions, even small ones, brings the scent of criticism and closed-mindedness into the room that can spoil an otherwise productive brainstorming session.
- Encourage note-taking. If quantity is the goal—and it should be—forcing people to wait for a turn to speak, or to wait for the facilitator to write it on the whiteboard, is an agonizingly slow way to go about things. If you're concerned about people keeping ideas to themselves, try handing out sticky notes or index cards for notes to be periodically collected and added to a shared display.

CREATE STRUCTURE

To get the writing done, you'll need a clear *structure* to support your writing work. You'll want to turn your assignment into a to-do list of sorts that helps you see what kind of *writing*-writing work actually needs to happen.

There are three documentation structures that can guide your next phase: outlines, templates, and inventories.

Outlines

Outlines are great for longform writing like product overviews, knowledge base articles, in-product documentation, and so on. Outlines give an...uh...well, an outline of what you need to communicate and the rough order in which you need to communicate it.

Creating an outline may give you flashbacks to school research papers, but they are very useful in the world of design writing. Outlines are hierarchical: main point, sub-point, sub-sub-point (**FIG 1.3**). In that way, the outline not only informs your writing, but also the design—the big idea becomes your H1, the next level your H2. Blocks of similar ideas at the same level might work well as bullet points or a chart.

List out the main beats, the big ideas, of what you want to say. Then, as you're able, add detail under those big ideas. Answer questions like: Who cares? So what? Why does this matter? Don't worry about how the words sound—the text of the outline is for you, not your readers.

After you've gotten your rough outline together, look for opportunities to group and collapse related ideas. Where are you repeating yourself? Where might you need to add a larger point to tie a few of the smaller ones together? Give a thought to the order of things, too. What information will be most useful to have toward the top of the copy? What can wait until the end?

Clear thinking is powerful. With a strong outline, some of your writing will seem to write itself!

New version announcement post

- Headline (simple and clear) [70 characters max]
    - announcing a new version of the app...
- Sub-head [150 characters max]
    - all new design, several great new features
- Introduction
    - a new version of the app is coming
    - it will be a paid upgrade
    - we're excited about it and hope you are too
- Body (headers + 1-3 paragraphs each)
    - Announcing the new version
        - It's true, we're finally releasing 3.0
        - We're most excited for: [something]
    - What's in the new version
        - now uses native cloud sync
            - will still work w/ Dropbox or G Drive
        - completely fresh design
        - imports old projects seamlessly
        - (link to full feature breakdown on product page)
    - What happens to the old version
        - nothing will change if you don't want it to
        - can upgrade and run both side-by-side
        - honoring all current support agreements
- Wrap-up
    - Call out and link to developer blog
    - See a preview here [product page]
- Promo area (inset)
    - Sign up to be notified
    - Email capture

FIG 1.3: An outline reflects both the shape of your ideas and the shape of your interface. In this example, the top level of the outline is used to mark out different sections of content within the post.

Templates

Templates are any tool that says "Structure your writing in this particular way." Content strategists have all kinds of names for the templates they make: page tables, page description diagrams, content templates, and more. Templates are sometimes built into content management systems or headless content systems like Gather Content.

Templates can generally be understood as a two-column table (**FIG 1.4**). The left column defines what needs to be written (including constraints like word or character limits), and the right column provides space to write the thing. You can turn any design that needs words into a template by simply listing the various design elements down the left column.

As the name implies, templates are a great choice when you have to make the same sort of thing more than once.

Meta Info	
Browser Title (visible in address bar and search results)	
URL Slug (trailing end of page URL)	
External search description (reader-friendly description of page content for search results previews)	
Social share description(s)	
Internal search description	

Product Header Area	
Product full name Include required ® or ™ or other marks.	
Product URL	
Support URL	
Plain-language description Not a slogan or tagline. Write a meaningful, clear, one sentence description for a general audience. No links. 200 characters.	
Positioning headline Key message in headline format. 200 characters.	
Features/Body One to three paragraphs. Links okay. Bullets okay if bookended by paragraph text. 800 characters.	
PDF brochure URL Optional	
Marketing video URL Optional	

FIG 1.4: A template with descriptions of what's needed on the left, and room for copy on the right, allows you to "fill in" your writing assignment as you go. It's easily extendable with additional columns to add things like approvals, translations, metadata, and more.

Inventories

Inventories work well when you have lots of little bits of texts, as with interface copy. Inventories are made in spreadsheets, where it's easy to keep track of all those little bits and their associated data.

You can start by sequentially numbering text elements in a wireframe—this creates a quick inventory that connects what's been designed and what's being written (**FIG 1.5**).

The resulting identification system makes it easier to manage your work and collaborate on it with others. Having all of your strings ID'd makes them "talkable"—the difference between:

	A	B	C	D	E
1	**ID**	**Element Type**	**Description**	**Text**	**Notes**
2	2.x	screen	sign-up screen	*n/a*	
3	2.0	headline	form header	Create Your Account	
4	**username**				
5	2.1	label	username entry	Username:	
6	2.1.1	field placeholder	username entry	Be friendly! Other users will see this.	
7	2.1.2a	validation error	too short	Usernames must be at least 5 characters.	
8	2.1.2b	validation error	special characters	Usernames can only include letters and numbers.	
9	2.1.2c	validation error	restricted	Sorry, that name is not available.	e.g. admin, AwesomeCo
10	**password**				
11	2.2	label	password entry	Choose a password:	
12	2.2.1	field placeholder	password entry	At least 8 characters.	
13	2.2.2a	validation error	password too short	Too short!	
14	2.2.2b	validation error	banned list	Try something more complicated.	e.g. password, 12345678
15	2.2.2b	validation error	invalid password message	Sorry, that's not working	
16	**zip**				
17	2.3	label	zip code	Your ZIP:	
18	2.3.1	field placeholder	zip code	e.g. 90210	(not validated/required)
19	2.7	text	existing account sign in	Already have an account? [Sign in.]	link second sentence
20	2.8	button	continue button	Create Account	grayed out until username + password validate
21	2.9	return key	keyboard form submit	Continue	UIReturnKeyType
22					
23					
24					

FIG 1.5: A spreadsheet inventory helps you track every string you need for an interface, and gives you room to capture all of the error states and alternative messages that might not fit neatly into a high-fidelity design mockup.

"Do you have the approved copy for G 7.1?"

and:

"Do you have the approved copy for the text that goes under the button on the fifth screen of the third section of the app? No, not that button, the other button. Right. Wait, that doesn't fit, what version are you looking at?"

MAKE SPACE TO WRITE

We're almost to the writing part of writing! To create your draft copy, you'll need three things: a place to put the words, a place to put yourself, and some time to do the writing.

Prepare your digital space

Thanks to our friends Copy and Paste, you can usually do your writing in one environment and move it to another without too much fuss. You don't have to do all of your writing in Microsoft Word or the CMS just because that's where it needs to end up.

You want a writing environment that thinks about writing the way that you do. It should make it easy for you to write quickly. It should make it easy for you to collaborate with others and complete editing and review steps in your workflow. And it should be appropriate to the type of content you're working on—a word processor focused on desktop publishing might well be overkill for writing out a few strings for your interface.

Web-based writing environments can be fantastic, and offer advantages when it comes to version control and collaboration. Be cautious about doing your work in a web browser, however. There are many points of potential failure: web browser crashes, service outages, accidental refreshes—you get the idea. (I don't think I'll ever break the habit of mashing ⌘S after finishing a paragraph.)

Consider a workflow where the bulk of your composing—those big sprints of "doing the writing"—happens in a stable local application on your computer. You can then copy your work into whatever web-based tool you need to use for editing. We'll talk about this more with version management in Chapter 3.

Your design environment might work well as a writing environment. If you go that route, create a duplicate version of your project before you start, so you've got the freedom to be a bit messy. Once you've got some final, authoritative text, you can drop it back into the master file in place of those squiggly lines.

Prepare your physical space

I once worked in a small, open-plan office at a startup company. Our designer, Amanda, took to wearing her "design hoodie" on days when she had to get a lot of work done. When the hood was up, we weren't allowed to bother her for any reason. No "quick questions." No "Have you seen that video where..." Hood up = DESIGN TIME, no interruptions.

Whether it's a hoodie or an office with a door or a coffee shop where no one knows you, it helps to do the writing in a space where you won't be interrupted. Developers and designers know that there are some kinds of work that require you to build a bit of intellectual momentum, and that being interrupted, even briefly, can kill that momentum. Writing is that kind of work, too.

This is challenging in some office cultures. Strive for it anyway. Try talking to your supervisor or project managers about ways to carve out the time and space you need to write. If writing is an infrequent responsibility and you have a lot of demands on your time, you may end up needing to shift your schedule a bit. Try writing early in the morning or late in the day when other folks are less likely to use your ears as an inbox.

Oh, and in case it needs saying: when it's time to write, turn off notifications on as many things as you can get away with. If closing your email client or shutting off your phone gives you anxiety, try a timer—the world's not going to end if you're offline for fifteen minutes. And if it does, look on the bright side: no more deadlines!

Clear (some of) your calendar

"Hey Siri, add appointment to write all the things from 1 p.m. to 3 p.m. tomorrow."

Blocking off time on your calendar to write—and protecting that time against meetings and interruptions—is a good start, and more than many writers are able to pull off. So do it if you can.

But be honest with yourself about that time. Two hours on the calendar rarely equals two nonstop hours of writing. (If you figure out how to do that, please tell me.)

Timeboxing can help you make the most of your writing time. Make a quick list of what you want to work on in a given period, and apportion each item some of that time. You could do this per screen or page (e.g., landing page, thirty minutes), by content type (e.g., confirmation buttons, twenty minutes), by user journey (e.g., password reset flow, thirty minutes), or whatever else makes sense for your brain and your assignment.

FIRST DRAFT INBOUND

Preparation isn't the part of writing that people tend to think of as writing, but it's no less important. Having a clear assignment, lots of inputs and ideas to work with, and a sense of how the rest of your work is going to go sets you up for a more efficient process and successful writing outcomes.

For the marketing copy on a new, large website, you might spend weeks in the Prepare phase. For the interface language on a single app screen, twenty or thirty minutes of preparation might be enough. A little planning up front goes a long way.

Take a breather if you need to, and get ready for the phase with all of the typing and crying: Compose.

COMPOSE

IT'S TIME TO COMPOSE YOURSELF! Err, your draft, that is.

The work you'll do in this phase is what most people refer to when they talk about writing—never mind all that pesky planning and editing work, right?

I told you earlier that writing isn't magic, but that doesn't mean we can't use a few tricks to make it easier. Those tricks revolve around two objectives: to write quickly and to write everything.

WRITE QUICKLY

I want you to write quickly, for two reasons:

1. If you try to compose the perfect draft one perfect word at a time, you'll never get the writing done.
2. Good clear writing comes from good clear thinking. The less time your thoughts have to rattle around in your head, the more time they can spend in the clear light of day—and the better they'll sound in your design.

Do a rough-in

One way to write quickly is to do as little writing as possible. Start with a *rough-in*: grab all of the relevant text from your inputs, and put it on or near where it needs to go in your design (FIG 2.1).

If there's one slot for a user testimonial, for instance, and you have a few to choose from, grab several that might work and drop them into that box. If you need to write labels for a tabbed navigation element, go ahead and drop in the simplest and most obvious label for each. A navigation bar that reads "Home | user stuff | promo stuff | settings and options" has you a lot further along already than "Label | label | label | label."

The sooner you move away from squiggly lines and *lorem ipsum*, the sooner you can get the writing done. A good rough-in lets you skip right past blank-page paralysis to *re*-writing, which goes a lot faster.

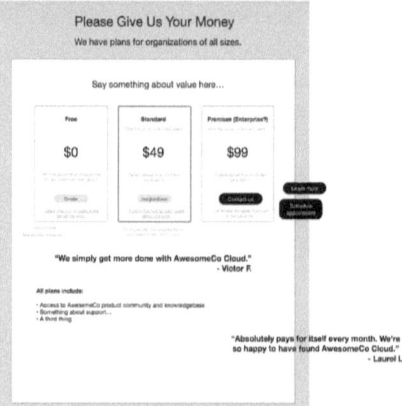

FIG 2.1: While both of these are unfinished, the wireframe on the right, with roughed-in copy, gives a much better idea of what the page is about—and what still needs to be written.

Use a scratchpad

If you had to suffer through standardized tests, you might already be familiar with paper scratchpads. A *scratchpad* is anything that helps you separate THE THING (i.e. your working draft) from NOT THE THING (everything else).

A digital scratchpad helps you write quickly because you're never stuck staring at a blinking cursor. You can jot out a mini outline in the scratchpad, or move text that's not working into the scratchpad and try again. I'll often cut and paste the text from my rough-in over to the scratchpad as I go, then refer to it while I'm writing true draft copy.

Scratchpads can also provide minor version control. Since I cut and paste sentences from my draft to my scratchpad instead of deleting them completely, I'm less likely to accidentally lose something. Having alternative text tucked away in your scratchpad can also help if the first review of your work doesn't go so great.

Don't forget that you're allowed to use actual paper, too. It's amazing how helpful it can be to jot a few words down on paper when you're having trouble maintaining momentum with your keyboard.

Skip the details

The things we need to write often include facts, figures, and statistics that we don't have readily at hand. And sometimes we run up against something that doesn't exist yet, like a link that hasn't been created or a product that hasn't been named.

In these situations, it's okay—preferable, even—to use a placeholder. Drop something in that will call attention to itself later and keep writing. DO NOT OPEN WIKIPEDIA. DO NOT POST IN SLACK. DO NOT ASK SIRI. Just keep writing.

Journalists use "TK" as a placeholder, which means "to come"—the unusual letter combination makes it easy to find-and-replace later. I myself use NARF, Pinky's catchphrase—yes, as in *Pinky and the Brain*—for the same reason. I also do a lot of ad hoc marking of things to follow up on, like // fix this later // or [NARF add link here].

If your writing environment is also a design environment, you might want to set off placeholders in another color or style. Whatever you do, pick something that's hard to miss during editing—just do it quickly and keep writing.

Reduce friction

Try to notice what causes frustration, slowdowns, or distractions while you're writing. A small irritation in your writing boots can add up to a hike-ending blister after an hour or two on the composing trail.

If you find yourself fussing with fonts and formatting before all the words are written, consider writing in a low-fidelity environment like a text editor.

If your writing environment's guidance (like automatic spelling correction, capitalization, lists, and styling) are getting in your way, turn 'em off! These little demons can make composing a draft feel like a game of Whac-A-Mole. There's a time and a place to check your spelling, style your quotes, and indent lists properly, and it's not now.

Finally, I recommend adopting a "lazy" mentality and occasionally asking yourself if there's a faster or automated way to do what you're about to do. Do you need to write this feature description from scratch, or can you borrow one from elsewhere in the app? Do you need to type that obnoxious CamelCase™ product name every time, or can you create a keyboard shortcut to format it automatically?

WRITE EVERYTHING

If you're still lost on how to start or what to write, you may need to revisit your inputs and assignment. But more than likely, at this point, you just need to start writing.

Pick something easy to get your fingers moving. (You don't have to start at the beginning.) Continue writing, and get the whole thing written before you start perfecting individual parts of it. Editing comes later, and besides, what you write in one area might impact what you write in another area.

You may want to track your progress against your outline, template, or inventory by crossing things out or changing colors after you've got something covered.

Write one thing at a time

The best way to write also generates the best kind of writing: say just one thing at a time. Say one thing in your headings. Say one thing on your buttons. Say one thing in the tooltip text, one thing in the error message, one thing in each paragraph.

Writers get stuck (and readers get lost) when the words are trying to express too much at once. Words are powerful, yes, but still bound by pesky constraints like "time" and "how brains work."

If you're feeling overwhelmed, or the words are coming slowly, narrow your scope. Focus in and say just one thing.

Practice your ACBs

The ACBs are a set of writing and editing lenses created by Ken Rand in his book *The 10% Solution*. The acronym stands for Accuracy, Clarity, and Brevity. The order of the lenses is as important as the lenses themselves.

Accuracy

Start by writing something that is objectively true. The labels in our interface copy need to correspond with what actually happens when the user interacts with those elements. The features and benefits in our marketing copy need to reflect the actual product the user is signing up for, not an imagined or ideal version. The product copy needs to provide real, useful guidance. If what we're writing is wrong, we're already sunk.

Accuracy in interface copy requires understanding how the interface actually behaves. If you're not sure, ask! You might be surprised how often you'll discover a button, link, or other element whose behavior is a mystery, even if you designed it. Find the answer, design the answer, or carve those unknowns out of the scope of your current assignment (and be sure to flag them for follow-up). A simple example: don't write DELETE (the file from the system) when you really mean REMOVE (the file from the list).

Accuracy in product copy often depends on understanding your reader's context. Something that's true for users that are signed in, for instance, might not be true for users that aren't. For your first draft, write out what you think is true to the best of your understanding, and flag anything that you think might need more attention.

Accuracy in marketing copy can be trickier. Stakeholders are often pushing for superlatives—the latest, greatest, best, most amazing. But accuracy isn't just about the truth; it's also a way to cut through the fluff and express more powerful and compelling ideas. For example, let's say you're editing a list of features for a new product and come across this:

> *Secure storage means you'll never have to worry about someone else accessing your important files.*

Not bad, but let's apply our accuracy lens and see what happens. We might ask: "Is it true that users will *never* have to worry about this? It is true that it's secure? What does *secure* mean? Is it true that no one else will *ever* access the files? Does that include our support department?"

Statements that *feel* accurate to your product and marketing teams aren't always objective statements of truth. What's secure to one person might be risky to another, and your product can't control what people will or won't worry about.

So let's say you look back at your inputs, and it turns out that your company uses an industry-leading encryption protocol, enables two-factor authentication by default, and has undergone a vigorous auditing process conducted by a well-respected outside agency. Nice! So instead of the (not objectively true) marketing text, you might write:

> *The most secure file storage solution our industry has ever seen.*

And that could be punched up even more with links to information about your security practices and so on. A big change and a powerful improvement, all from one little question: Is this true?

Clarity

After you have your facts straight, you want to focus on making your writing clear—that is, straightforward, simple, and easy to understand.

To create clarity, look for opportunities to:

- replace resplendently fantastical fancy language with simpler language (and uncommon words with common ones)
- put things in a logical order
- add supporting information
- add examples and anecdotes to reinforce your point

- delete things that don't support your main idea
- define concepts that users might be unfamiliar with

Context is also an important part of clarity. Take a fresh look at the context-creating inputs from your Prepare phase to make sure that the text you've prepared will be readily understood by your audience.

Sometimes the easiest way to bring clarity to your writing is to simply rewrite it. Unlike in real life, where whatever stupid thing that just came out of your mouth at the party can never be unsaid, writing allows for instant do-overs. You don't owe anything to your first draft (except accuracy, of course).

(Rewrites are a balancing act. You want to keep writing, and write quickly, yes. And you want to leave the bulk of your editing work for the next phase. But in practice, doing the writing tends to involve quick iterative cycles of writing something and then revising what you've just written.)

Clarity is in the middle of this ACB sandwich because text can never be clear if it's not accurate or too brief.

Brevity

Brevity is last—it's admirable, but it should never cause you to sacrifice accuracy or clarity. *Short* doesn't automatically mean easier to read or understand.

When I was a UX writer on a design team, I consulted daily with designers who were stuck because they *started* with brevity. Sometimes they were trying to write text directly within the confines of a wireframe (and without accurate character constraints). Other times, a well-intentioned but ill-informed stakeholder was pushing them to "make it shorter," because that's the only advice they knew about writing for the web.

"How do I make it fit?" is the right question at the wrong time. Start by writing out a complete idea, *then* refine and trim. For instance, you might start with:

> *Click this button to submit the information in the form and also join our mailing list.*

That's obviously quite lengthy and not good. But it's written! And it's something to work from, as opposed to the nothing you had before. Another quick pass—focusing on the verbs—might get you down to:

Submit and Join

That's more concise, but also sounds like the slogan of a sci-fi totalitarian regime. But it has the key information, and gives you a foundation for further revision.

Laying out messages like that for an entire screen or flow puts the whole story in front of you—which makes what you need to say, and where, much more apparent. For instance, after writing just that little bit, you might realize that submitting the form and joining the mailing list should be separate options, requiring a checkbox and message below the button. Mark it for discussion and move on to the next bit of writing—there's no reason to perfect the text of a button that might change.

KEEP WRITING

If this were a longer book, I could muddle your mind with all kinds of additional tips and tricks and hacks and methods for "doing" the writing. But it might be for the best that this isn't a longer book. No matter how many tricks you employ, the only thing that really gets that first draft done is you making the clickity-clackity sound on your keyboard.

Write quickly, with tools that make writing easier, in an environment conducive to getting the writing done. Repeat this until you've written a decent, complete draft that meets the requirements of your assignment.

Drafts can be rough. They might be messy. But some of it, hopefully, is good and smart—maybe even brilliant. But the draft is just the start. Next? We Edit.

3

EDIT

THERE'S A BIT OF A FUZZY LINE between composing and editing. Often, to reach that complete first draft, we'll cut and paste words and phrases, rewrite ideas, maybe even scratch a whole screen's worth of text and start over.

This is inevitable, though perhaps not ideal. "Tweaking" the text while we write will catch errors and improve phrasing, but it won't elevate the consistency, clarity, and quality of the writing.

For our purposes, *editing* is about substantively improving the writing. Don't confuse this with proofreading, where you fix typos and punctuation. That stuff is important, too, but comes at the end of the process, which is why we'll talk more about it in the next chapter.

The mental shift from writing to editing doesn't happen automatically. If you've just finished your first big run through the Compose phase, job one is to take a break. Not too long, mind you. A lunch break will do. A walk around the block. A hoverboard trip to the all-you-can-eat activated yogurt buffet, if you work in one of those futuristic Silicon Valley offices.

Going somewhere, changing your workspace, or otherwise physically marking a shift in mindset allows you to sit down to your work with a fresh intention. This helps you focus on what you're doing right now: editing, editing, editing.

And hands off that Delete key! There's something important we need to cover first: ch-ch-ch-ch-changes.

TRACK YOUR CHANGES

Moving from composing text to editing text means that you'll have *versions*. There's the first version, and then the version after you correct that obvious spelling mistake, and the version after you rewrite the headline, and so on. Every change creates a new version of the text. Add collaborators and other editors to the mix, and suddenly there are versions of your versions. And versions of those versions!

You need an anchor in this version storm: a system to track and manage revisions before you begin editing. Whether you're revising a single error message string inside a web app, or trying to put some polish on a thirty-page white paper, the principles are the same:

- You want to preserve your first draft for reference.
- You want to be able to undo (and redo) changes that you and others make to the text with relative ease.
- You want to keep track of the who and the why of any changes more seriously than correcting typos and spelling errors.

Editing can be dangerous. Move too quickly, and you can lose the thread of what you were trying to accomplish—or lose good work altogether. It's like a big gust of wind blowing loose papers off an old-timey novelist's desk straight into the fireplace, except in this case you're the wind *and* the fire. (The paper was your chance at leaving early today.)

Tracking this stuff is especially important if you're doing lots of fast loops (say, in Agile-ish environments) where sign-offs happen incrementally. You don't want your text to surprise anyone the next time they look at it. And if they *are* surprised, you'll want to be able to explain and defend your choices.

There are as many methods of managing versions as there are teams and workflows. Let's look at a few of the more common ones.

Haxonomies

Haxonomy is a fancy name for a simple thing you're probably already doing somewhere. The name is a portmanteau of *hack* and *taxonomy*. A taxonomy, in the general sense, is a method of classification. When the type of organization you want isn't available where you want it, you can "hack" it in. Hence: haxonomy.

Many people instinctively manage document versions with haxonomies in the file name. This leads to names like:

2018-02-28 Big Deliverable Version 5 FINAL copy ACTUAL FINAL—SK + KH Edits.docx.PDF

Instead, plan your haxonomies. Some useful file-naming patterns include:

- An incremental number system (like V1, V2, V3, etc.), updated each time *before* you make any substantive changes to the text—the biggest number will always be the most recent version.
- Initials to indicate whose edits the version contains (e.g., Book Draft—SK).
- Shorthand for process steps that have been completed, such as "LGL" for a version of the text that the lawyers have already signed off on.

Where you store files can communicate information, too—for instance, making the canonical version of the text the only file allowed in a particular shared folder.

It's best not to improvise these things. Without a clear plan, shared by the whole team, things like color codes and tags and folders will turn into a noisy mess.

Changelogs

Changelogs are just what they sound like: a written log of changes that have been published or otherwise incorporated into the thing that's been changed.

Changelogs are a concept you can use on any project, no fancy software required. You could even keep one right at the top of the document itself. Having the history of the writing paired closely *with* the writing makes it easier for everyone to understand how the text ended up the way that it did.

This is especially handy during reviews with persnickety stakeholders who try to poke holes in your process:

> Stakeholder: *"Where is this writing coming from? Has marketing looked at this?"*
> You (so on top of version management): *"Why, yes, you can see that on June 19, we had a collaborative working session on the text with marketing."*
> Stakeholder: *"Hmm. Well. Okay, good."*

Make notes about what you change as you change it, and include dates. This is tedious, yes, but gets less so over time as you build the habit and get used to the benefits.

Here are some example entries you might put in a manual changelog:

- *02/13 DN—Wrote first draft based on outline from support team*
- *02/17 MJM—Revised all CTA strings based on style guide (incl. title case on buttons)*
- *2/18 DN—Completely new intro copy dropped at VP's request*
- *2/25 (PM update email)—Reviewed by support (Maurice) for accuracy, gave okay*

You may think you'll remember these types of things, but you won't. Pairing your changelog with a basic versioning system will make it *much* easier to navigate all of the forthcoming trickiness of getting text reviewed and approved.

Automatic version control

Online environments like Google Documents and features like Track Changes in Microsoft Word do a decent job of highlighting what's different since the last time you looked at the text, but they can't read your mind. If the editing process takes you through several deeply different versions of the text—different conceptual approaches, a different tone, a different structure—it can be hard to return to a specific, earlier approach.

Don't rely exclusively on autosaves and cloud backups—documenting decisions and intent are as much a part of smart version control as monitoring changes to the text itself.

If you work with code, you might already be a version control pro with a tool like GitHub. These types of systems are great for knowing exactly what changed and when, but the "why" is still up to you: be sure to comment on those commits.

KNOW WHY YOU'RE EDITING

Editing requires an intention, a lens of sorts—an answer to the question "Editing for what?" You could rewrite a draft fifty times, but if you don't have a goal in mind during those rewrites, how can you know whether it's getting any better? Having a lens changes your mindset from merely *reading* the text to *evaluating* the text against particular criteria. Let's look at a few of the more common editing lenses.

Focus

Editing to make your writing more focused means cutting out stuff that isn't related to the key goals and messages of your design. Writing is focused when every word—*every* word—is serving a clear purpose.

When you edit for focus, you might start by skimming through the text and marking any words that seem incidental, frivolous, trivial, or disconnected. Ask yourself what, if anything, they're contributing to the writing. If you don't have a good answer, cut it.

Editing for focus can also mean evaluating your text against your stated goals. How well does it articulate the key messages? If the goal is to sell, is it compelling and persuasive? If the goal is to educate, is it clear and complete? Does it anticipate and answer key questions?

Simplicity

Everyone will tell you that simplicity is a good thing. But how do you actually achieve it? If you feel like the writing is too complex and could benefit from being simpler, there are three key levers you can manipulate:

- **Structure:** How it's organized. Things that feel complex often feel simpler once they're in the right order. It's the same information, mostly the same words, but organized in a way that adds context and clarifies the meaning.

- **Language:** The words you use. Many organizations strive to apply principles of plain language to their writing—using the simplest words possible in any given situation. Plain language doesn't mean dumbed-down or boring; directness and clarity make room for your big ideas to pop.
- **Concept:** The big idea behind the writing. Clear concepts keep things simple. If you're explaining something new or complex, consider a metaphor that's relatable for your primary audience.

Readability

Is the writing easy or hard to read? Is it easy or hard to understand? Can people follow along, or will they get lost?

Readability isn't about *legibility* in the design sense, but about what's happening in a reader's head as they process the words.

If we want our writing to be readable and user-friendly, we need to do more work now so that our readers have less work to do later. For instance:

- Extract the most important point and put it right at the top.
- Clearly specify the next action the reader needs to take.
- State whom the information is for (or not for).
- Vary the lengths of sentences and paragraphs. (Rhythmic variety is easier to read.)

Readability tests can help evaluate your text based on things like overall length and the number of syllables in your words. While not a foolproof metric, it's useful for comparing newer versions of text with older ones to see if you're headed in the right direction. You could also benchmark against similar text within your design, or within a competitor's design. For some recommended readability tools, see the Resources section.

Consistency

Editing for consistency means making sure your writing agrees with itself, and that it agrees with all of the other stuff it's connected to. Little inconsistencies creep in everywhere: here it's the "welcome" screen, there it's the "sign-in" screen. Here it's a "free trial," there it's a "test drive." The button on this contact form says "Submit," but that one says "Send."

Part of your job is to ensure that the words you use to describe product features and interface components are consistent throughout the experience. One way to achieve this is through the application of a *controlled vocabulary*.

Controlled vocabularies are like custom dictionaries. They can exist as a simple list of terms and definitions; you could even incorporate them as a layer in a design pattern library.

Editing for consistency is fairly straightforward, provided you have controlled vocabulary documentation or an interface element inventory. Use the search function within your writing environment to find the listed terms—or the terms the list is meant to replace.

Strength

Do the words make an impact? Does the writing feel strong, or does it feel passive? Passive voice is almost guaranteed to suck the strength out of your writing.

To eliminate passive voice, you first have to recognize it. Talking about subjects and objects and diagramming sentences is boring, so let's say: passive voice has no ownership—it feels weak—whereas active voice takes a stand—it feels strong.

Compare, for instance:

- **Passive voice:** "Mistakes were made."
- **Active voice:** "I screwed up. My bad."

In the passive example, no one is *doing* anything. It's weak. Who made the mistakes? No one, apparently. Passive voice isn't wrong, per se, but it has less impact than active voice. In active voice, there's *action*, not just *existence*.

Putting your ideas in the right order also adds impact and strength. In a first draft, you're figuring out what to write as you're writing it, which means that the most interesting idea—the one with the most impact—often ends up at the end of your sentence, paragraph, or flow. Move it to the top, and *boom*! Writing so strong, it's flexing for selfies.

Tone

Getting the right tone for your writing means that it's emotionally appropriate to the audience and subject matter. It's about finding the right "vibe," the right "level" for the writing.

With a clear assignment to guide you (meaning you know the audience and context for your writing), odds are good that your tone is already fairly appropriate. Still, tone can be a useful editing lens on a screen-by-screen or paragraph-by-paragraph basis. Just like in real life, one inappropriate comment at the wrong moment can throw off an entire experience.

There are a few specific angles on tone that often apply to business and design writing. Let's take a closer look.

Urgency

Buy now! Ends soon! Subscribe in the next thirty seconds or there will never be rainbows again!

Creating a sense of urgency can be useful, but, when done poorly, risks ringing hollow and making users skeptical. It can even do long-term damage to whether or not users trust you and your brand. Urgency must be applied appropriately.

Not appropriate:

> *URGENT! ATTENTION REQUIRED! We value your feedback. If you do not respond to our previous survey in the next 3 days, you will LOSE your ability to be entered into a contest with 8 million other customers to win a single $25 Outback Steakhouse Gift Certificate.*

Better:

> *URGENT! ATTENTION REQUIRED! Your domain will expire in 3 days. It is NOT set to renew. If you do not manually renew, you could lose access to your domain name forever.*

Be thoughtful about your writing's necessary level of urgency. Sometimes the right thing to do is to slow people down. Sometimes the right thing to do *is* to freak them out (just a little). Get clear on what's appropriate for your design, and edit accordingly.

Scale

Editing for appropriate scale means asking yourself how important the subject really is, and communicating that importance accurately and effectively.

Hyperbole is a crutch. Calling everything the *biggest, best, greatest,* and *most fantastic ever* is the sign of a weak mind. A weak, orange, treasonous mind.

Not every product update is revolutionary. Not every feature is groundbreaking. Are you expressing a big idea or a small idea? Does everyone *need* to stop in their tracks and pay attention to this, or is it okay if it only reaches some users?

Emotion

The emotional aspect of your writing needs to be appropriate to the subject matter. Delight and humor can be wonderful things, but they shouldn't be shoved into every experience. It's perfectly fine for some experiences—and the writing that supports them—to be serious, clear, or even somber.

Timing is a critical factor in conveying the appropriate emotion with your writing. For instance, users don't want cutesy messages while their mortgage payment is being processed.

The earlier prep work you've done to understand your audience and the context of the design writing will go a long way toward helping you convey the appropriate emotional tone with your words. It may be worth revisiting that information ahead of an editing pass to put you in an audience-focused state of mind.

DO THE EDITING

At this point, you might be asking: how exactly do I *do* the editing?

To effectively edit your writing, you need to introduce a layer of abstraction between you and the copy. (If you've ever flipped text in a design upside-down to check the kerning, you know what I'm talking about.)

That abstraction layer can be a hack, a tool, or another person (like an editor)—whatever you need to approach the work with more distance and objectivity.

Choose editing tools that make you look closely and carefully at the actual words that have been written, not just your impression of what it *says*. These are a few methods that work reliably, no matter what you've written.

Read it

At the risk of stating the obvious: it's a good idea to read what you've written before you show it to someone else. This readback will help you catch major errors like unfinished sentences and big copy-and-paste goofs.

The problem with reading, however, is that you're very good at it. Too good! You've been reading your whole life, and as with anything you've practiced that much, a lot of it happens on autopilot. Your pattern-optimized brain (thanks, evolution!) wants to make sense of whatever mess of letters it encounters, and it will lie, cheat, and steal to make that happen.

That means that a quiet, in-your-head readback is not a great way to catch some of the more pernicious errors of grammar, spelling, and formatting that will plague your copy. There are smarter approaches to reading your work that will help you edit. Let's look at a few.

Read it out loud

Reading your text out loud (into the air, making actual sounds with your mouth) is one of the most recommended bits of editing advice for writers.

However, I know from experience that if I simply tell you to read it out loud, you'll think to yourself, "Oh, yes, that is very good advice. I will read my writing out loud from now on." But then you won't actually do it. You're not going to do it!

Why don't people do it? Lots of reasons, I suppose. It takes too long? It feels silly? You work in an open-plan office (a.k.a. Writer's Hell) and it would bug your coworkers?

Still, if it's a very important piece, *do* try hard to read it out loud at a normal speaking pace. You can print your text and take it on a walk (don't forget a red pen!). Or slip into an unused conference room. I sometimes read my text "out loud" to myself at a very low volume.

While you're reading, listen. Listen for anywhere that you trip up, anything that sounds funny, anything that's hard to say, anywhere that you got lost. Mark those passages and consider them for revision.

Read it out loud to a person

This is especially good for marketing copy. Remember, real human people are going to have to read what you write. If you can't read it out loud to someone without feeling completely awkward, that's pretty telling.

There's also something magical about "performing" your text for someone—it engages a very different part of the brain. You may well surprise yourself with a creative improvisation as you're speaking the words that wouldn't have occurred to you as you were writing them.

(And yes, you can totally read it to your dog. That has the added benefit of being *adorable*.)

Have the computer read it to you

Text-to-speech is a wonderful accessibility tool, and just so happens to be handy for writers, too. I frequently make my Mac read things back to me. In many apps, you can highlight the text you want read and select a read-aloud option, and the computer will read absolutely everything in the most literal way. This is great for catching repeated words and other typos that your brain might trick you into thinking aren't there.

Have a person read it to you

Having someone else read it out loud makes the feedback very direct. Readers who are not you might put the emphasis in unexpected places, revealing potential ambiguities. You can hear where they hesitate and where they speed up. You don't even have to ask them for their thoughts (though you might as well)—just hearing them read it will reveal plenty.

Ask for feedback

Stakeholder reviews—for both design and writing—are often built into our processes. What doesn't occur to many writers, however, is that they may be able to ask stakeholders for *feedback* before asking them for *approval*.

This may be a new idea for your stakeholders, too, and thus needs to be approached carefully. How you frame your invitation matters. Dropping a meeting invite on someone's calendar called "Review onboarding text" sets a very different tone than sending a message asking if you can borrow a few minutes of their time at the end of the day to run some preliminary approaches by them.

Be clear what kind of feedback you're looking for, and ask specific questions. For example:

- *Does this include all of the information we need to communicate to customers?*
- *We're trying out a lighthearted tone. How would you feel if the final draft ends up sounding something like this?*
- *I'm focusing on structure right now. Is this the right order to tell this story?*
- *I want to know what questions you think customers will have after reading this.*

It helps to articulate for stakeholders where you are in the process, and to assure them that, yes, they'll have a chance to see the final text, yes, it's going to go through legal, yes, someone is going to proofread it, yes, they can see it before it goes live on the website, etc.

While careful framing helps, it won't work for everyone. You may simply have to grin and bear it while they circle typos and missing ™ symbols. Other stakeholders will insist on seeing the writing in the design, or in the browser, or on paper—consider which delivery method will solicit useful feedback from the stakeholder in question. (And you'll eventually learn that some people just can't help you, no matter how you frame it.)

If you make changes based on the feedback, or just get unstuck, be sure to note that in your changelog, and let your collaborator know that they contributed. (Never assume that a stakeholder will remember what they told you when it comes time to approve the final text. Keep your receipts!)

Collaborate with others

Sometimes, for whatever reason, you just can't quite figure out how to say what you're trying to say. Or you've said it, and it's blah. Time to bring in a fresh pair of eyes.

Collaborating with colleagues can be one of the quickest and most effective ways to help you get unstuck—or to unsuck a particularly rough passage. Even brief conversations can yield big outcomes.

A handy framing device for these collaborations is to ask, "How would you approach this?" That's more freeing than "What's the best way to write this?" and more forward-looking than "What's wrong with this?"

Build a buddy system with other writers so you can bounce text off of each other regularly. Fellow designers can be collaborators, too—they can help you tease out whether you're looking at a design problem, a writing problem, a product problem, or something else entirely. Running your drafts past coworkers also creates opportunities to learn from each other and to increase consistency in language and terminology.

LOCK IT IN

Sometimes, the hardest part about editing is stopping. It can feel like there's always more to improve upon, more people you should run the copy by, more of the word count you should trim away.

This is part of why we plan our writing workflow—editing rarely feels "done," but if we've completed our workflow steps, it's done *enough*. Eventually, you have to say: "This is the text. These are the words. We are moving forward with these words."

You might not be there yet, and that's okay. If editing helped you identify some gaps, you might need to move back to composing. If the text still feels really rough, you might need to add additional editing steps, or find a friend to help. And if it's all a big mess, you might need to re-evaluate your assignment and prepare a fresh plan to get the writing done.

Eventually, though, you'll be able to lock in your draft. If your writing assignment were a term paper, at this point you'd be able to hit Send (and then hit the bar…or the gym, or the beach, or the slopes, I don't know your jam.). But in the world of design writing, we're not done yet. To get the writing really and truly done, you have to Finish.

FINISH

WRITING IN A DESIGN CONTEXT can feel like stepping in quicksand—not *real* quicksand, but 1980s cinematic quicksand that swallows children whole in seconds. Luckily, you've already got a trusty whip—or vine, or long docile snake...whatever your preferred method of quicksand escape may be. That whip is the assignment.

Clearly articulating the assignment, as we did in the Prepare phase, lets you know when you can finally put your pencil down and step away from the role of writer, *even and especially if the design itself is not yet done.*

This last phase, Finish, includes all of the steps big and small you need to take care of to complete your writing assignment, including approvals, hand-offs, reintegrating it into the design, and reflecting on your work.

GETTING THE WRITING APPROVED

Most of the things we write for a design project will be subject to review and approval by someone else—a design lead, a product owner, a business stakeholder. Whether the text is reviewed and approved together with the full design, or separately, or some combination thereof, will depend on your design project and organizational culture.

It's hard to get anyone to pay attention to anything, let alone to get busy stakeholders to slow down and *read* something, carefully and critically. Like anything else you design, part of your job is to sell and present your work. Luckily, all of the skills you have for presenting design work apply to presenting your writing.

If you're bringing writing for review for the first time, try to find a coworker who's already gone through the process, and ask their advice. Ask about any quirks or preferences of the people who will be doing the reviewing, and how they give feedback. Some stakeholders need a little translation. I worked at a place once where hearing the CEO say "I don't completely hate this" was cause for celebration, and a profanity-laden tirade often just meant "This needs a bit more work." Colorful guy!

You will want to anticipate stakeholder questions, prepare answers to those questions, and present those answers in a sensible order before they have a chance to ask them. And I do mean *present*—you will be best served by holding a meeting and walking people through this information, rather than firing off a draft over email and hoping for the best.

As the writer, there are some things you'll want to be prepared for during these final approvals. They will probably be familiar from your experience as a designer:

- **The swoop and poop:** Just what it sounds like—somebody swoops in and takes a shit all over everything you've written. A clear assignment and a well-maintained changelog can help serve as your shit umbrella, since sometimes the pooping is motivated by a mistaken belief that everything about the writing is arbitrary. Identifying important stakeholders early and integrating them into your process can help alleviate this; people are less likely to shit on something if they feel like they were part of making it.
- **Goalpost shifting:** You wrote the text to accomplish X, and yet someone is complaining that it doesn't do Y. They're evaluating your writing against a different (or more ambitious) goal. It could be that the project's goals have changed; it could also be that they are having a flight of fancy, or pre-launch jitters. Again, diligence in the Prepare phase (and a good project manager) will help you navigate these conversations.
- **Scope and role creep:** This is anything that puts you on the hook for more work beyond what everyone agreed to at the beginning. You might be able to guess what I'm going to suggest now as a remedy: diligence in the Prepare phase. Fight these battles early on to articulate a clear role and clear assignment. This helps you avoid looking like the defensive jerk who can't be a team player toward the end.

DO THE FINISH WORK

Most of the trades (think: plumbing, carpentry, painting, woodworking) draw a distinction between *rough work* and *finish work*.

Finish work is all the stuff you save until the very end to make sure you won't have to redo it. There's little sense in painting the drywall if you still have to cut a bunch of holes in it to install the electrical.

If you follow the workflow laid out in this book, you will naturally accumulate a list of finish work for your writing. Review your assignment, your draft, and your project notes to compile a fresh checklist of what needs to happen to really be *done*.

Let's look at a few common steps that are best left until the tail end of your writing workflow.

Add links

While you're writing and editing, there are likely links that you want (or *have*) to include in order to make the design function. In earlier phases, you marked those link opportunities, but didn't actually link them, in order to keep your momentum.

But we're not composing anymore, so it's time to find your sources and write those links. First, review your writing for the links you marked, as well as new link opportunities. Some link behavior, like on interface elements such as buttons, has probably been spelled out in the design. For longer informational pieces, like knowledge base articles and blog posts, additional links can increase the usefulness of what you've created.

There's a bit of an art form to linking, especially in longform text. Before social media swallowed the web, there was a very egalitarian spirit of linking any mention of a concept to a good source about that topic. I try to carry that spirit forward in my digital writing, when I can. (Worst case: somebody downstream removes the link.)

Here are some quick guidelines to help you add good links:

- Link complete phrases and ideas. The linked text should make its destination clear (no point in being mysterious).
- Link to the thing the first time it's mentioned in the writing. (It doesn't need to be linked every time.)
- Link to things that support the goals of your design. You don't need to link every noun that your site has a web page for. Consider why readers are looking at that page at all, and what they'll get out of following the link—and whether navigating away to a different page will disrupt a more critical action.
- If the link does anything weird like open a dialog, download a file, reload the page, or open a new window, think very carefully about why that's the case, and include as much context around the link as possible. Your style guide or usability guidelines may have advice on this.

Write and add metadata

As the writer, you're more familiar with the content than anyone else will ever be. This puts you in a good position to decide (or at least recommend) things like appropriate tags and categories, the best place within your site structure to publish the content, and so on. You're also in a good position to write summaries for search engines and social media.

Ideally, you're writing something that's based on a predetermined content type, with all of the metadata required to support that content type already spelled out in advance. In practice, you may find yourself needing to ask questions and poke around inside of systems to determine what metadata is needed.

To oversimplify things, there's going to be two kinds of metadata: public and process. *Public metadata* means stuff that a user or reader might end up seeing, like a page title, search engine summary, author name, or blog category. Public metadata tends to be easier to write at the end of your workflow, since it's based on the final content of whatever you wrote.

Process metadata is stuff that helps your content move through the production workflow, like ID numbers that correspond to a content inventory, or status indicators to track who's reviewed and signed off on the content. You'll need to package all of this stuff up together along with your writing in order to cross that assignment off your to-do list.

Proof it

Proofreading your final drafts is a smart habit to get into, even if what you've written will go through its own dedicated proofing and QA process. Proofing your own writing will help you catch any silly mistakes you'd rather other people not see first, and it helps you learn about your own bad habits and improve upon them.

Make sure the quotation marks are smart, copyright symbols are in place, paragraphs break where you intended, and so on. If you've been working in plain text or otherwise keeping your drafts tidy and clean, you may not have much to clean up. Still, be sure to check for any formatting funkiness and hidden characters that happened while copying and pasting your text into another format.

To guide this process, consider using a personal proofing list: a playbook of sorts for your proofreading process. The list contains words (or parts of words) and phrases that you can search for in your text using the Find feature in your writing environment. It's not a list of dos and don'ts—it's just about seeing your text in a fresh way to make it easier to catch errors.

Some things you might put on your list:

- words you frequently misspell (the misspelled version would go on your list)
- homonyms that trip you up
- typos you can't seem to shake (like "teh")
- marketing and business jargon you want to avoid
- misspellings of product and feature names relevant to your design
- words that represent key topics or pages you want to make sure get linked

- word parts like "ly" and "ing" that can highlight potentially weak writing
- words that are not the preferred synonym for something in your product universe (e.g., if members should "join" instead of "register," you'd put "register" on your list—you can check your controlled vocabulary documentation for things like this.)

You might also include specific steps you want to go through each time before you hand off a draft, such as saving a master copy, alerting someone on your team, or applying formatting that's needed to shepherd it along the project process.

PREPARE FOR THE FUTURE

In addition to the requirements of your assignment and production workflow, there are some personal tasks you'll want to complete to support yourself as a writer and designer. They add some finality to the process, and over time will make it easier for you to get the writing done in the future.

Tidy your desk

Remember how I told you to keep the receipts? Keep that up. Grab a clean copy of that final version and put it in a safe deposit box, so to speak. You want a version that represents every design decision that was made up until the text was out of your hands.

This is to cover your ass, yes, and to save for your portfolio, yes—but it's also because you don't want to have to do anything over again if something gets screwed up when you're no longer minding the store. Projects can stall, stakeholders can leave, designers and developers can screw up. Hopefully you won't ever need your safe deposit copy, but you'll be damn glad to have it if you do.

This is a good habit to get into even if *you* are the next step in the design process. Having a safe copy of the text can help you recover from bad ghost edits—those tiny little changes that you just can't help yourself from making while moving the text from one place to another. Even if it feels minor, you'll want to be able to know what changed from the approved version so you can roll it back if needed.

Keep everything you've written, even if it got thrashed to pieces during editing or review. All that stuff you wrote during this assignment can serve as an input for you on the next assignment. Mindmaps, interview notes, and alternate earlier drafts can all be very valuable.

Write down what you've learned

Writing, like any other thing you might want to get better at, benefits from reflection and review.

So. How did it go?

Whether you use a formal postmortem process with multiple participants, or just a bit of "Remember this next time" journaling on your own, you should reflect on a few key things:

- What changed between articulating and finishing the writing assignment? Why?
- What tools worked well? What tools didn't work well? Why?
- How could you have gotten this work done faster?
- How could you have improved the quality of the writing?
- What do you wish you'd known at the beginning that you know now?
- What is the number one thing you would do differently next time?

There are also a few housekeeping items you'll want to take care of:

- Reflect on the editing phase and update your personal proofing list.

- Send updates and quick notes of thanks to anyone who contributed to the writing, if appropriate (such as SMEs you interviewed and editors you collaborated with).
- Check your various to-do apps and project management tools to make sure everything is checked off.
- Ensure that whoever needed the writing is aware that it's done and ready to roll!

HIT SEND AND BUY YOURSELF A LEGO SET

The absolute last step in all of this—and absolutely do not skip this—is to celebrate. For a big or difficult assignment, I celebrate finishing my work by buying a LEGO set. For smaller assignments, it might be a pint of ice cream. (Note that this is celebration ice cream, distinct from any ice cream consumed while working on the assignment.)

Whether it's ice cream or a LEGO set or going for a run along the river, having a celebration ritual reinforces the idea that you're *done* with the thing and helps move it along out of your brain. Rituals are a way of telling yourself: "The assignment is finished, and I did my best. Good job, me."

Your next writing assignment might be easier, or harder, or bigger, or smaller. I hope you've learned from this experience that you can always get the writing done with a good plan and a bit of perseverance, and by following the four key phases: Prepare, Compose, Edit, and, finally, Finish.

It's a lot to manage, I know. If you find yourself feeling overwhelmed along the way, remember these truths:

1. Writing is part of design. (And being a designer!)
2. Writing is always hard. (I feel your pain.)
3. Workflow gets the writing done. (It ain't magic, just planning.)
4. You can write. (And you did!)

Good job, you!

ACKNOWLEDGMENTS

Writing a book about writing makes one feel especially vulnerable. I couldn't have done it without the skillful guidance, warm encouragement, and A+ edits that Lisa Maria Martin and Katel LeDû provided throughout this process. Thank you Jeffrey Zeldman, Jason Santa Maria, and everyone else at A Book Apart for creating a world where this book can exist alongside so many great titles I rely on in my own work.

I'm honored and grateful to have Dan Brown's name on my cover. He gives generously to the design community in myriad ways and I've grown so much from following his work. I personally recommend reading anything and everything he writes.

To my family, especially Mom, Dad, Aunt Vandie, Uncle George, Jake, and Rob, thank you for your love, and for supporting my early interest in computers and the web, even if you didn't always understand what I was going on about. Thanks Mom and Dad for all the books, all the trips to the library, and for making sure we had a home computer and internet access long before either was common in rural Nebraska.

Many ideas in this book were first developed for a conference talk and workshop. To everyone who shared their time with me in those sessions, asked challenging questions, and provided feedback, thank you.

I'm grateful to everyone who was ever patient with me while I fumbled about trying to figure out my career, especially Fritz Jünker, Amedeo Rossi, Ryan Patrick, Keri Thien, Cat Rocketship, Kathy Landin Hellstern, Neil Roberts, Igor Dobrosavljević, Amanda Morrow, Dan Newman, Agnieszka Skuczynska, and Sara Briddell. I'm still not sure what I want to do when I grow up, but I'm closer thanks to all of you.

To Michael Metts, thank you for your friendship, your encouragement on this project, and for indulging me in various schemes over the years.

Part of everything good I've ever done is for Soro and Gweedo. I miss you both.

Finally, to Kristina Halvorson and my Brain Traffic and Confab family, thank you for making a place for me. I literally and figuratively do not know where I would be without you.

RESOURCES

Sorry, friend, no magic tricks in this section, either. But I *do* have some apps, tools, and further reading that can make the writing work a bit easier (or at least more fun).

Digital writing environments

It's a golden age for writing apps, especially on Mac. Most are relatively inexpensive, especially compared to the big box "productivity suites" of the past. Try out a few to find one that fits your style.

Environments for writing solo

- Drafts (iOS, soon on macOS) is a great place for quickly capturing and manipulating text.
- Ulysses (macOS and iOS) uses a library model (as opposed to files), making it a good place to develop longer writing like blog posts, white papers, and ebooks.
- Byword (macOS and iOS) has a clean and simple plain text writing environment that makes it a nice upgrade from TextEdit.

Environments for writing together

- Google Drive is hard to beat for collaborative writing.
- Dropbox Paper is an alternative to Google.
- Draft is a web-based writing environment focused on version control and collaboration. If I need detailed feedback from one collaborator and don't want to set up a whole new thing, I might drop text into Draft and share it that way.

Reading to improve your writing

Books

- *The Elements of Style* is a surprisingly enjoyable and inspiring read about expressing oneself clearly. It's a classic for a reason.
- *The 10% Solution* is an uncommon little book focused on self-editing your writing. The author brings to bear a perspective on writing for broadcast (e.g., radio commercials) and there are a surprising number of parallels to writing for digital.
- *The Yahoo! Style Guide* has a good chance of outlasting the Yahoo! company. It contains excellent guidance on a number of conventions unique to writing for the web and digital interfaces. When in doubt, I default to the advice in this book.
- *Letting Go of the Words* offers lots of case studies and examples that might inspire your own work writing longform website content.
- *Content Design* would be a great book to pick up right after this one, if you have a lot of content to create. It has simple and clear guidance on how to connect business needs with audience needs in all of your content, and some process tips on approaching text-heavy pages with a design mindset.

Articles

- "The Grammar of Interactivity" introduced me to the "Wilty Wilt test" for evaluating the clarity of interface copy.
- Mary Dash's writing advice on plainlanguage.gov covers a lot of good stuff on active vs. passive voice, modifiers, verb choice, and other writerly matters I didn't get into in this brief text.

Useful utilities

- Pastebot is a clipboard manager that puts multiple levels of copy-and-paste right under your fingers, even allowing you to save frequently used snippets.
- TextExpander is a text replacement app—like autocorrect, except actually useful. Type a few characters and *bloop!* they get automatically expanded into something else. (For instance, ;sig expands my email signature.) Great for adding consistency to anything you have to type frequently, like URLs, email addresses, and product names.
- Readable.io is an online tool focused on readability tests. You can also run readability tests in Word or in an app like Marked 2. (Remember to use the same readability test in the same app throughout your assignment to ensure accurate results.)
- Terminology is a zippy and well-designed pocket thesaurus/dictionary. I find this app especially useful when I know what word I want but I can't quite think of it. Great for "namestorming" sessions for products and features, too.

Mindmapping and idea sorting

Mindmapping is a popular app category and there are plenty to choose from. There may be mindmapping functionality built into design software that you already own.

- MindNode (macOS and iOS) is my preferred bare-bones outlining and mindmapping app. I use it on almost every project. I also like to eat peanut butter straight out of the jar. So, you know, it may be best to try out a few and make up your own, uh, mind.
- MindMeister (Web, iOS, Android) is a collaboration-focused mindmapping and diagramming platform.
- OmniGraffle (macOS and iOS) is a simple diagramming tool that can rough out concepts quickly—and make mindmaps in a pinch.
- Trello (Web) is my favorite way to digitally approximate a fresh pack of index cards.

Markdown mastery

Markdown is a popular plain text syntax for writing that's destined for the web—you can quickly mark bulleted lists, headings, and more without having to remove your hands from the keyboard.

- What is Markdown? site by Kirk Strobeck is a good one-stop-shop online guide for understanding Markdown.
- "Markdown: Basics" on Daring Fireball is an introductory guide to the syntax from one of its creators.
- Marked 2 (MacOS) is an incredible Swiss Army knife for web writers. The built-in proofing tools can help highlight weak writing and automate your personal proofing list, and the ability to preview with custom stylesheets makes it easy to "wireframe" pages with just text.
- The Markdown Service Tools by Brett Terpstra are the closest you'll get to a magic trick. Service tools install at the system level, and these in particular allow you to do really handy stuff with text in nearly any application, like automatically cleaning up list formatting, or creating Markdown links from all of your current Safari tabs.

REFERENCES

Shortened URLs are numbered sequentially; the related long URLs are listed below for reference.

Chapter 3

03-01 https://www.plainlanguage.gov/
03-02 http://unsuck-it.com/

Chapter 4

04-01 https://abookapart.com/products/design-is-a-job

Resources

05-01 http://getdrafts.com/
05-02 https://ulysses.app/
05-03 https://bywordapp.com/
05-04 https://drive.google.com/drive/u/0/
05-05 http://paper.dropbox.com/
05-06 https://draftin.com/
05-07 https://www.goodreads.com/book/show/33514.The_Elements_of_Style
05-08 http://www.fairwoodpress.com/catalog/item/7652154/8139852.htm
05-09 https://www.goodreads.com/book/show/6883650-the-yahoo-style-guide
05-10 https://www.goodreads.com/book/show/1135441.Letting_Go_of_the_Words
05-11 https://contentdesign.london/book/
05-12 http://www.uxbooth.com/articles/the-grammar-of-interactivity/
05-13 https://www.plainlanguage.gov/resources/articles/dash-writing-tips/

05-14 https://tapbots.com/pastebot/
05-15 https://textexpander.com/
05-16 https://readable.io/
05-17 https://support.office.com/en-us/article/test-your-document-s-readability-85b4969e-e80a-4777-8dd3-f7fc3c8b3fd2
05-18 https://agiletortoise.com/terminology/
05-19 https://mindnode.com/
05-20 https://www.mindmeister.com/
05-21 https://www.omnigroup.com/omnigraffle
05-22 http://www.trello.com/
05-23 http://kirkstrobeck.github.io/whatismarkdown.com/
05-24 https://daringfireball.net/projects/markdown/basics
05-25 http://marked2app.com/
05-26 http://brettterpstra.com/projects/markdown-service-tools

INDEX

A

ACBs 29
accuracy 29

B

brainstorming 16
brevity 31

C

changelogs 36-37
clarity 30-31
collaboration 46
context 10, 31

D

Dash, Mary 59
deadline 10
digital space 20-21

E

editing 34
    consistency 39-40
    focus 38
    readability 39
    simplicity 38
    strength 40
    tone 41

F

feedback 45-46
file-naming 36
finish work 51
freewriting 14-15

G

generating ideas 12-16
getting approval 49-50

H

haxonomy 35-36

I

inputs 11-12
inventories 19

L

LEGO 56
links 51-52

M

metadata 52-53
mindmapping 13

N

NARF 27

O

outlines 17-18

P

physical space 21-22
preparation 9
proofreading 53-54

R

Rand, Ken 29
requirements 10
roles 10
rough-in 25

S

scope 10
scratchpad 26
Strobeck, Kirk 61
structure 17-20

T

templates 18-19
Terpstra, Brett 61
TK 27
track changes 34

V

version control 37
versions 34
voice
    active 40
    passive 40

W

Wilty Wilt test 59
workflow 4-5
writing assignment 9-10

ABOUT A BOOK APART

We cover the emerging and essential topics in web design and development with style, clarity, and above all, brevity—because working designer-developers can't afford to waste time.

COLOPHON

The text is set in FF Yoga and its companion, FF Yoga Sans, both by Xavier Dupré. Headlines and cover are set in Titling Gothic by David Berlow.

ABOUT THE AUTHOR

Scott Kubie is a designer and digital strategist living in Minneapolis, where he works as lead content strategist at Brain Traffic. His first bit of published writing was a fan letter in the LEGO catalog. Scott can be found online at kubie.co and in person at various grungy rock clubs around the Twin Cities.

Since 2010, Scott has delivered over sixty public talks and workshops on writing, content strategy, and user experience design for audiences of designers, developers, marketers, artists, makers, and more. He loves a good framework and finding ways to make esoteric design topics a bit more practical.